World of Farming

Seasons on a Farm

Nancy Dickmann

Raintree

www.raintreepublishers.co.uk
Visit our website to find out
more information about
Raintree books.

To order:

☎ Phone 0845 6044371

📄 Fax +44 (0) 1865 312263

📧 Email myorders@raintreepublishers.co.uk

Customers from outside the UK please telephone +44 1865 312262

Raintree is an imprint of Capstone Global Library Limited, a company incorporated in England and Wales having its registered office at 7 Pilgrim Street, London, EC4V 6LB – Registered company number: 6695582

Text © Capstone Global Library Limited 2011
First published in hardback in 2011
The moral rights of the proprietor have been asserted.

Edited by Siân Smith, Nancy Dickmann, and Rebecca Rissman
Designed by Joanna Hinton-Malivoire
Picture research by Mica Brancic
Production by Victoria Fitzgerald
Originated by Capstone Global Library Ltd
Colour reproduction by Dot Gradations Ltd, UK
Printed and bound in China by South China Printing Company Ltd

ISBN 978 0 431 19558 2
15 14 13 12 11 10
10 9 8 7 6 5 4 3 2 1

British Library Cataloguing in Publication Data
Dickmann, Nancy.
    Seasons on a farm. -- (World of farming)
    1. Farm life--Pictorial works--Juvenile literature.
    2. Seasons--Pictorial works--Juvenile literature.
    I. Title II. Series
    630-dc22

Acknowledgements
We would like to thank the following for permission to reproduce photographs: Corbis pp.**7** (© Image Source), **17** (zefa Select/© Awilli), **22** (zefa Select/© Awilli); Getty Images pp.**18** (Comstock/Jupiter Images), **20**, **23 bottom** (Dorling Kindersley/Alan Buckingham); Photolibrary pp.**4** (Digital Light Source/Sergio Izquierdo), **5** (imagebroker.net/Michael Krabs), **6** (Britain On View/Chris Laurens), **8** (Reso/Diaphor La Phototheque), **9** (F1Online RF/Sodapix Sodapix), **10** (Robert Harding Travel/Ann & Steve Toon), **11** (Juniors Bildarchiv), **12** (Index Stock Imagery/Inga Spence), **13** (Neil Duncan), **14** (Tips Italia/Bildagentur RM), **15** (age fotostock/Alan Kearney), **16** (Digital Light Source/Richard Hutchings), **19** (Nordic Photos/Mikael Andersson), **21**, **23 middle** (All Canada Photos/Don Weixl), **23 top** (Britain On View/Chris Laurens).

Front cover photograph of strawberries being harvested reproduced with permission of Shutterstock (© Boris Khamitsevich). Back cover photograph of a ewe with lamb in Scotland reproduced with permission of Photolibrary (Robert Harding Travel/Ann & Steve Toon).

The publisher would like to thank Dee Reid, Diana Bentley, and Nancy Harris for their invaluable help with this book.

Contents

What is a farm? 4

Spring. 6

Summer 12

Autumn 14

Winter .18

Can you remember? 22

Picture glossary 23

Index 24

What is a farm?

sweetcorn

A farm is a place where food is grown.

Farms change with the seasons.

Spring

plough

In spring, farmers plough the fields.

They get the fields ready for planting.

seeds

In spring, farmers plant seeds.

The seeds will grow into plants.

In spring, lambs are born.

In spring, calves are born.

Summer

In summer, the plants grow taller.

The farmer waters the plants.

Autumn

In autumn, the plants are ready
to pick.

Farmers collect the wheat.

In autumn, farmers pick apples.

hay

Farmers make hay to feed their animals.

Winter

In winter, farmers repair their
farm machines.

Farmers make sure their animals stay warm.

seeds

In winter, farmers buy seeds to plant next year.

The farm gets ready for spring.

Can you remember?

What do farmers make hay for?

Answer on page 24

Picture glossary

 **plough** farm tool that breaks up the ground so that farmers can plant seeds

 **season** a time of the year. Spring, summer, autumn, and winter are seasons.

 **seed** plants grow from seeds. Farmers plant seeds in the ground.

Index

animals 10, 11, 17, 19

autumn 14, 16

seeds 8, 9, 20

spring 6, 8, 10, 11, 21

summer 12

winter 18, 20

Answer to quiz on page 22: Farmers make hay so that they can feed it to their animals.

Notes to parents and teachers

Before reading

Ask the children to name the four seasons and look at a calendar to agree when these seasons happen. What is the weather like in the different seasons?

After reading

• Make a circular picture of the seasons on a farm together. Divide a large circle of paper into quarters and split the class into four groups. Give each group a season and ask them to draw pictures of what happens on the farm in that season. Get them to cut out the pictures and stick them on their quarter of the circle and display the finished picture on the classroom wall.

• Talk about when the fruits and vegetables that grow where you live are ready to eat. Make a frieze showing each month of the year and use books and the Internet together to find out when local foods are ready to harvest. Get the children to draw these fruits and vegetables and stick them on the correct month. Talk about how some foods can be stored so we can eat them during the winter. Try to eat some of these seasonal foods together each month.